IN THE COMPANY OF THE MUSE

Dike Okoro

IN THE COMPANY OF THE MUSE

Cissus World Press Poetry Series

DIKE OKORO

II

Publisher's information, address:
Cissus World Press, P.O.Box 240865, Milwaukee, WI 53224
WWW.Cissusworldpress.com

First published in the U.S.A by Cissus World Press

Cover Design/Photo: Dike Okoro
First Published 2015
ISBN   978-0967951126

CISSUS WORLD PRESS BOOKS are published by Dike Okoro,
Founding Publisher

Acknowledgments

Full of Crow Poetry - "She"
The Caribbean Writer - "After Edwidge Danticat" & "Rituals"
Witness Magazine - "What Song in this World is Without Sorrow?"
We Have Crossed Many Rivers: New Poetry from Africa - "A Tribute to Mother", "Homeland" & "Orashi River"
Indiana Voice Journal (Poetry) - "Confirmation", "Don't forget" & "Lagos, night"
Ken Again Magazine - "Song of Proclamation"

Also by Dike Okoro

Dance of the Heart
Weeping Shadows
We Have Crossed Many Rivers: New Poetry from Africa
(Editor)
Speaking for the Generations: Contemporary Short Stories
from Africa (Editor)
Two Zulu Poets: Mazisi Kunene and BW Vilakazi
(Selected and Edited)
Songs for Wonodi: An International Anthology of Poems
(Editor)
Echoes from the Mountain: Selected Poems by Mazisi Kunene
(Editor)
Reflections on Mazisi Kunene (Essays and Interviews)

IN THE COMPANY OF THE MUSE

For Okechukwu:
Of blessed memory

"A word has power in and of itself. It comes from nothing into sound and meaning; it gives origin to all things." -N. Scott Momaday, The Way to Rainy Mountain

There are, it may be, so many
kinds of voices in the world, and
none of them is without signification.
--I Corinthians 14: 10

Contents

I

II

I

HOMELAND

Your soil knows my feet,
your fruits know my teeth.

Your rivers know my skin,
your sun knows my face.

Your streets crowd my dreams,
your tears flow from my eyes.

Your hopes revive my joy,
your trials incite my prayers.

I the bird hatched from your nest,
the fish that swam in your waters

when the waves were free of flotsam.
I lift up my eyes to the sky &

not a forgotten memory rises
from the wind's burning skirt.

Only undulations of encomiums
await your expected return;

you whose journey to the sacred hills
invokes my thrill but keeps me awake,

as I ponder in different ways but
remember in one way, waiting,

waiting
for you!

IN THE COMPANY OF THE MUSE

In the company of the muse
I am a bird needing sunlight to fly

in the company of the muse
I am a rooster waiting on sunrise to crow

in the company of the muse
I am a canoe trusting my paddler to move

in the company of the muse
I am a seed needing the soil to sprout

in the company of the muse
I am the flower trusting sunlight to be alive

in the company of the muse
I am the fisherman lucky to catch fish with a torn net

in the company of the muse
I am the swimmer who is part of the water's memory

in the company of the muse
I am a tree ambushed by the rain yet tolerant of nature's ploy

in the company of the muse
I am a river green from slime yet the pride of the morning bathers.

NOSTALGIA

The Orashi River's tales resurrect memories of home songs
Relieving me of aching trails of passions that will not leave.

I smell the river's breath & long for the shores again,
The inroad to the water world of childhood's mornings

When fishermen reveling in stories of night's passing
Adjust their legs on canoe & revive hope in nets held tight.

The Orashi River's tales resurrect memories of home songs
& I must be alone in sacred tidings with the muse.

Horizons of blue sky break in the mind as I find reason
To surrender to echoes of waves and talkative winds;

It is the point of greatness I recollect, Orashi,
Emblem of lust now a figment of rusty waste

Where once depended the swimmers' world
And the fisherman's invocation, until time's irony

Presented itself at the altar of stinginess & abandon;
Pretentious guardians of our sacred earth & their wily ways,

& a pitiful awakening now defines your once powerful face,
The evocative waters tumbling, giving hope to lost dreams.

POEM FOR EZEKIEL

Nights in my childhood were framed in adult-composed folktales from the animal
Kingdom, with themed morals meant to teach the young right from wrong.

I wish the same for you in this expectant love nest where drums and dances treat the mind to
rhythms even I have suddenly become alien to as a result of distance.

Today I make a pact with my future to take you there, the famed land many,
Myself included, left in search of treasures in the snow, while being forgetful of

The fact that love is indiscriminate and can grow anywhere, regardless of soil,
Coast or clime. It is fifteen years now since my feet felt the pulse of the earth

At home, a spiritual disconnect I never envision you experiencing, since I know
You carry a heart that reminds me of your grandfather and a humility I compare

To your grandmother's. The elders say no one ever loses where he or she comes from,
So long as the mind and the tongue are never strangers to the treasured items of one's

Heritage. So I pray you remember the songs I shall teach you and keep their flavored words
Evoking trees, birds, rivers, creeks, ponds, fish and the sky, for when you choose to

Celebrate in the open those things common some fail to recognize for their value, you
Intuitively recreate in the mind gifts returning as blessings.

KEN-SARO WIWA

When the news of the hangman's crime
Met my eyes in a newspaper in Chicago
I shrugged silently
And shook my head
To resist the cry of defeat

Ken, even in death
Your name echoes the courageous journey
You took to remind us why
Fearlessness in the face of adversity
Means victory to those who refuse to keep silent
When facing the nozzle of a gun

Today I have listened to the wind
How many times I do not remember
But with each sound came a thrilling voice
One of a fearless orator and freedom fighter
Whose end at the gallows
Birthed a testimony for our generation

To sing the sin of oil greed
While displaying the valiant stride
That liberates the human spirit.

OBI WALI

The day the cock ready to crow flapped its wings,
Opened its mouth but could not crow

The day the sun shone a deep orange red and yet
Nobody noticed the brightness in the sky

The day the town crier beat a gong all over the city
Of Port Harcourt and nobody heard his message

The day the fisherman stood tired and yet waited,
Hoping to take home the reward of a heavy net

The day the hunter came face to face with death
While trying to separate a buffalo from a deathtrap

The day the thief stopped to trace from a familiar path
The road to the execution party of his own father

The day the bushfire claimed the forest despite the
Sudden downpour that filled the gutters and drains

The day the redneck lizard jumped off a wall and landed,
Forgetting to engage in head nodding

That was the day assassins stole into your bedroom, Obi,
To rob a generation of the gifts of your heart songs.

Dr. Obi Wali, of Ikwerre ethnic nationality, was murdered, butchered, and dismembered
in his bedroom by hired assassins on 26 April 1993. A respected Senator and one of the
founding fathers of Rivers State, he is the author of the controversial and lauded essay,
"The dead end of African literature."

I STILL REMEMBER HIM

for Nna, after twenty four years

He loved to run errands
Only three but wise beyond his years

Beloved by all tenants in the yard
But the bellicose fate threw him a curveball

That afternoon I hid under the bed
Thinking a bomb had blasted outside

Only to look out the window seconds later
As the kid, naked, skin peeled from head to toe,

Jumped up and down on sand,
Shouting, I don die I don die o

By nightfall
Sympathizers

Camped
Outside his bedroom in the hospital

No doctors and nurses scurried around
Only family and friends watched, speechless

As his bed, shaped like a cross
To extend the thin material covering

Him from top
To bottom

Shielded air from penetrating
Skin charred and swollen

His silence all this while
Spoke
Very little of his courage
As I stared with outrage,

Unwilling to comprehend
Why a kid at three

Should be fated to
Go this way,

On a day a bird
Of doom sang

A mesmerizing song
To the absentminded

Whose fingers
Scratched the

Matchbox
In a bedroom also

A storage for a
Leaking gas cylinder.

Note: I don die o is I'm dying in Nigerian pidgin English.

BENTIU

Like Vladimir waiting for Godot, we waited for global
Intervention while Kigali was reborn. Churches
And mosques littered with corpses. Hospitals housing
Bodies, daring words to paint scenes with adjectives.
Was it worth it? This gorging of the present's brains to make an oil
Hub a habitat for tears? The dead decomposing heaped
On sand. Vultures hovering, then landing; their uninterrupted
Feast on abdomen and limbs an invitation the stray
Dogs found too enticing to ignore. Betraying the pen's
Desire to mate paper, I reposed silently, taking in
Lucky Dube's reminder: "It takes a million people
To build a good reputation, but
It takes one stupid fool to destroy
Everything they've done."

Bentiu: Oil city in South Sudan; venue of a terrorist
 attack in 2014, which left hundreds dead on the streets.
Lucky Dube: South Africa reggae singer who
achieved international recognition for his conscious lyrics.

AS HE LAY ON THE GROUND

---after a market mob attack turned gory
They bathed him with fuel,
his penis struck with wood covered with blood.
I nuh be thief he cried, looking heavenward.
Shut up! Nah today you go die, they replied.
I and my friends we watched, betraying
every cause to be human by keeping silent.
Later that day, circling a bonfire at the backyard,
we celebrated cowardice by retelling
the deed to our uninterested age mates,
unashamed we had done nothing to dare
danger & spare yet another life wasted
after accusations of petty robbery.
By morning, when the mournful sun rose,
we trekked to school, too absentminded
to recognize the ashes gathered
from yesterday's cadaver.

TREASURED MOMENTS

If the past is night I shall enter with a little boy's eyes, mine,
And scurry around treasured moments and sad stops.

Like my first holy communion, dressed in white shirt
And white pants. A saintly attire, I think now, recalling

The preparation to the glorious day. Holding mother's
Hands, barely six, we walked the market short cuts

Frequented by women in love with talking. Talking about
Their profits for the day. Talking about their husbands'

Escapades and dalliances. Talking about their love for God.
The unseen presence they honor in church on Sundays,

When dressed in their best outfits they seize the moment
To put in the offering basket a substantial amount from

The previous week's sales, trusting the road they find in faith
Will send their way a reward for meritorious service.

If the past is night I shall enter with my eyes shining like a burning
Candle guiding my way, as I hum like my grandfather, sit with

Arms folded like my father, my ears perking as the night news
Is relayed on WGN-TV, the evening's guide that combs the city,

Taking me through the tunnel of current events until the body
Becomes a tent that sleep wishes to claim for a period of time.

And when morning comes with its impatience, strutting by loudly,

I take from the noises on the streets the vagaries of memory

I trace to a quiet afternoon by my mother's grave site, with
The preacher saying his last words and older brother picking up

A shovel to spill sand over casket, answering to tradition's calling,
The planting of mother that left a hole in the fabric of family history.

FERRYING TO ROBBEN ISLAND

At last a dream long expected
has become a reality.
Everybody in the boat are shaking
Like wet clothes hung outside to dry.
There is the smell of water;
there is the evidence of joy
on white stones home to black ducks,
as we rush on water toward what had seemed
a patch of sand from a mountaintop,
but now looks everything the dreamer
dreams to see. Piece of land content at being
a hole in history's heart. The wings of a treasured bird
ever flight thirsty.

THE OLD COUPLE

I needed no one to tell me they've lived in the same house
before Adam knew Eve, or
that the flashes of smiles on their faces were doors
that opened to welcome the sojourner's gifts.
It happened many years ago
in a hotel in Durban, Kwazulu-natal
after I had helped the audience believe again
that birds could fly on pierced wings
and that kicking one's foot against a stone
should never be the defining chapter to our individual story.
A couple greyed.
A man dressed in cool brown suit;
a woman dressed in flowered gown,
holding flower.
Both sought my hand for a handshake.
Their showers of thanks for a poem I today
do not remember salutations I took to heart warmly
ever since I began to look to memories as windows of
monotonous voices.
Some we cherish; others we put on like clothes.
Like the adorable old couple i've refused to get off my mind.

FATHER

Thirteen mounds stared at the sun
in your mother's backyard
before your birth.
Today, I know why the elders say
your name unties knots
in the gathering of the brave.
This praise song is for you,
as you walk through the amazing
groves of old age.

IN MEMORIAM
for Mazisi Kunene

I have seen the great river,
the sacred water home to the chosen
whose light shone this way
and gave hope to the homeless children
and the deserted widows.
The birds sang over it,
the sun hung proudly over it,
the wind swung amid its presence
as if in pronouncement of that
which was plain to the naked eyes.

I have seen the great river,
home to the songs of those that passed
this way, home to the dreams of
those expected in future.
Standing at its shores,
waiting his turn
to be transported by its waves,
was the great bard. The one who
sung the fortune of your children, Africa;
the one who died pleading for the fate of
your children, Africa.

I have seen the great river,
where forgiveness takes refuge
and vengeance is held captive;
where the feet of humankind
is welcomed and all who stand
at its shores are children returning
to their mother's womb!

LETTER TO JUNE

And what if I sing of skies
And fingers drawing faces on sand,
Would you also label me
The tired artist searching
For a home where none exists?
And what if I broke my silence
In Madiba's cell and imagined
Brutus breaking stone
Under a sunny sky,
Would you also say I belong
To the category confined to histories?
Listen, I forged an alliance
With freedom years ago,
Borrowed a spoon from Shakespeare's table
And learned vanity's tough love
From Solomon.
So endear me to your heart, if
This play on words does not entice
You like a fresh wine, for
Only at the dying of a day,
Sometimes, do we find meaning
In praising the sun.

MOTHER'S ADVICE

Never laugh at the man who wakes up
Homeless in a town full of friends.

Always watch the ground as you walk,
For talking can also be a form of entrapment.

Arm yourself with a forgiving heart, for
The grave beckons the heart heavy with grudge.

NELSON MANDELA BRIDGE

Johannesburg's eye,
Madiba's thesis.

I rode a bicycle
over your riddled heart.

Crossing dignified
like Brooklyn's bridge.

UMLAZI

Somewhere
Among your mountains
A collision awaits memory.
I take from the experience
The liberty of knowing,
Since the past also births the present.

Umlazi: town in Durban, South Africa.

ROBBEN ISLAND

Let the drums beat. I have not come
to weep and sob over your past injustices.

Let the waves roar. I do not seek to remember
the hurt in stories exalting your irony.

But let the wind dance inexorably, for these eyes
desire the tree that survived in the desert's storm;

the keen bird's heart, adventurous like the sky, dreaming
like the vast sea;

the earth's patience, accommodating to all that steps
on its head, yet pleased with its allegiance to generosity.

There is a priceless possession in the names of heroes, an
ancient calling where truths prevail over brutes, and

the strangeness of histories lies, emotive emblems, are
gains vindicating victories enriching humanity!

Let your drums beat. I have not come
to weep and sob over past injustices.

Let the waves roar. I do not seek silence to remember
ironies today celebrated as victory!

Cape Town
2003

II

WHEN LOST IN THOUGHTS OF YOU
(for CJ)

Each morning we wake up next to each other
your smile transports me to a place I'd rather

be despite the heavy load of the previous day
that sags in my head. Your words, sonorous

in their own way, lift me up from sleep's quiet
world into a bright new day and I am at once

reassured of the singular vision that beautifies
the challenging journey of wedlock that binds us.

For these reasons, and for the seasons expected
to fortify our union, I shall navigate roads labeled

impassable and sing songs of liberation after every
turmoil avoided, knowing this favor you brought

into my life is but the warmth coming from love's
imperfect corner meant to give meaning to our world.

WHENEVER I RETURNED HOME

I read the smiles on a stranger's face meticulously.
Grandmother taught me a long time ago to
reserve a room occupied for trust and distrust,
anytime I returned home to revel in the
drumbeats of my ancestral land. And so,
in honoring her, I armed myself
with caution, deflecting every attempt
by the vile to point
at me in a crowd and say aloud
my granny's treasured name.
Today I remember my homeland
and sing quiet praises to God,
for bruises I do not see on my
skin, and for pot holes I avoided
in the dark, each evening I circled
the bush paths, alone under the crescent
moonlight, my pen and notebook in my bag,
my mind a map of poems desiring a writer.

TO MIRIAM ZENZILE MAKEBA

I have your name engraved somewhere
in the memory box i've carried in my heart
since a summer rain in 2003 sent me flying
to Jo'burg in search of you.
Strange how Nina Simone inspired the trip;
her painted lips, brown eyes and Afro,
metaphors I admired seeking you.
Her cries about life's troubles
my reasons for finding you.
When poeple talk about the bird
Whose nest cry globalized Sophiatown,
I see you. In Odetta's slave work songs
you lived; in Nina's jazz riffs you blossomed.
The blues married you because Biko's
spirit wouldn't sleep when you sang
of apartheid's teeth in freedom's flesh.
Axiom of our generation,
Madiba's antidote where hope's lost.
A letter came in this morning, Zenzile.
Its message a meticulously wrought epitaph
embalmed in a tribute to Paul Simon's Graceland.
Like your voice that made living a choice, not a perdition,
even when there seemed to be no hands lifting up the dying
and only a pounding heart assured them of tomorrow.

POEM FOR MADIBA

We have learned from your departure
the brief stay of true love & the uncanny
ways of forgiveness. Now we wait
for the full moon to entrust our hopes
to chance, so we can take from every risk
imaginable the humbling experience
of waiting to see again a smile like yours,
Madiba.

NANGA

Your eyes wear the leopard's dotted skin,
On your shoulder rests a load heavier than an elephant.
Close your mouth and I shall tell you why
Words are not mere playthings of the gods.
You say you are a shadow planted
Among mortals to revive the dream
Dreaming out itself in the orphan's cry,
But I say you dipped your feet in the water
Too soon, since night and day
Never run dry of tears, each
Moment you wander alone,
Your image repelling ghosts
A tribute to street gossip
And one mother's lamentation.

PROCLAMATION

Inspired by sky-bound glows at night, I built a palace of retreat
from where I watch the cosmos charm the earth

Inspired by water and air and wind and fire, I store memory
in the agencies of my living, day and night, to preserve my being

Inspired by ants promising their colony fortresses of
convocation
in storages hidden, I search soil and trees endlessly

Inspired by the sun whose story is always fiery
and heat-razed, I collect
healing potions from arrows of rains

Inspired by the mountain whose head is always
the eagles' hideout, I wait
for the plants crawling on boulders and
stones, sending up lessons to the sky

Inspired by the flutters entreating the eyes to
specter like butterflies in the sun,
I imagine silence the voice of the poem unwritten.

OF COURSE (for T.O.)

He threw a stone across a river
to win a horse race among princes.
Wordsmith of Urhobo lineage,
today the sun has shone your way
to remind all of what transpired this day.
I remember vividly Onobrakpeya's tale
ferried across great lands by a griot
tracking truth from the kingdom of songs.
Then the umbrellas of the sojourners kept
busy in the rain, and riddles melted
in the tongues of sages. Who knew then
that angels in disguise also belonged
to the gatherings of devils, the jesters
at the court of noble men and women
when the season of tears visits the brave
and their dreams are assaulted by graves
desiring caskets? But fortune is never
far from the reach of the hopeful—
this is the light held firmly by believers
where all have failed to make sense
while the eyes of those hopeful are
steadily focused on the sky.

*Bruce Obomeyoma Onobrakpeya is a painter and sculptor. He work has been exhibited
in Sweden, at the Tate Modern in London, and at the National Museum of African Art of
the Smithsonian Institution in Washington, USA.

BECAUSE I WAS THINKING OF YOU

I left a stone in a pond.

SOMETHING HAS HAPPENED TO THESE RIVERS

The coloring that steals words from the sage.
The tainted mirror that poisons the thirsty birds.
The fisherman takes from what he sees
the fingers of death professing troubles
for the days to come.
They bring bulldozers for the present's profit
but forget the healing balm for tomorrows' bruises.
I was at a gathering of birds with similar colors
where upon a rooster's crow summoned up
courage for song,
to read the eulogies of crude oil floating on water
to simulate that which was intended to be natural.
Our ways these days have gone care free.
We sing the boat and canoes but forget the waves;
we share the profits and boast of oil but forget
the killer air replicated in ignorance and pride.
Time was when as children we danced out of
excitement at seeing the rainbow on water.
But today future pain has given birth again
to wise thoughts dangerous for the ears of power.
But who dances in the open when the roof
under which he sleeps is on fire?
Something has happened to these rivers;
things so disturbing the sage refuses sleep
to wander in the musing deep.

MY SONG

The squirrel edits it
each moment it crushes the kernel,
the rooster sells it
each day it crows in pronouncement of dawn!
And now I wander in contentment,
my heart filled with the moon's ease,
my eyes desperate for dawn's blue cheek.
Nobody dances in the open anymore!
Snipers prowl the land,
their hearts eaters waiting on the meal of chance.
Once I promised to write a letter for tomorrow
but today's sorrows betray the heart's laughter.
I had thought the Tsunami was in Asia
until I found its nightmarish tears in my own backyard.
Drums of the forefathers washed ashore
and our voices forced into dirges.
Sandy from New Jersey, I stalked your rage
drooling over prayers in sleep for my brother
and his beautiful family from whose memory
I sang songs for the safeguarding of family fruits,
not knowing the Niger Delta suffered the ambush of fate,
the cycle now the a tale of legends in Pacqiao's land.
But we sing the seasons while we walk
as much as sing them while we talk.
A measure of hope taken
like the dependence on a rope
thrown over a wall
to ensure a safe crossing
unto paths that assure gifts and brighter days,
when the ground becomes uncomfortable
for standing
and shelter is sought in the rain.
My song,

this song I sing,
the squirrel edits it
to crush the kernel;
the rooster sells it
as it crows imperiously,
but this heart allows it to flow
over time's moments,
ladders determining life's stones.

CONFIRMATION

Now armed with the lessons of
Life, I carry with me

The sea and the sky
Wherever I go.

And when strangers ask
Why I labor the flesh

To resist fresh
Mistakes, I remind

Them that we all
Belong to the earth

And must fetch hope
From the sky's sunny home,

If we desire peace from
The sea within.

DON'T FORGET

When you plant a tree
You preserve your father's lineage

When you protect a river
You honor your mother's sacrifice

When you break bread with kisses,
You forgive hisses

When you shield from the heart worries
You prolong your life

These are not lines
For talks and walks,

But treasures reaffirming
Life's invaluable lessons.

LAGOS, NIGHT

For hours I stalked the sky's glows,
And since they pelted me with silence,
My heart wandered like the solo wind
On the deserted bridge.

The breezes fondled my eyelashes
For rough edges I never knew
I had, and vagrants,
Scuttling here and there
Like people running for cover in the rain,
Left more blames for time to name.

GENERAL HOSPITAL

Where the creepy stories are written
by simple acts that validate errors fatal
where the common man enters without a will
and if fortunate returns home with a head
still standing on his shoulders

general hospital

where the dogged physician only answers
to urgency when the nurse on duty
assures him money has been paid
where the rule is you are treated after you pay
to spare the gritty doctor the economy's bite

general hospital

where Cordelia went a year after childbirth
to tend to a stubborn headache's palaver
only to be sent home in a casket
after the surgeon on duty prayed forgiveness
for failing to operate on her brain properly

WHEN I STRAY IN THE DARK

After taking a momentary stroll into night's vast corridor
For escape, the minstrel gives a gentle nod in acknowledgement
Of the stars, in his heart an imaginary bell dangling.
Such moments he has known throughout his lifetime,
The nomadic adventures reviving the deep river of
Memory, the parts to quiet groves nobody sees but him.
He gathers the offerings of the dark, cricket songs he
Retains in memory like money pocketed,
To outlive dull moments; the distant
Smile of the dreaming moon, and the collar-tugging
Rough breeze he welcomes with heavy eyes,
Since the momentary stroll will launch him into surrender
To the muse once indoors and sitting alone, to conjure
Experiences that will liberate the heart.

I'D BE HAPPY

I'm a bird without wings
I need my family history to fly across oceans
I need the peace of the human family to calculate
The latitude of communal relationships

On my tongue rests my mood's choices
On my head sits an egg i'm still learning to protect
I've the song of my dead mother as my guide
I've the tears of my living father as my caution

It takes a tree seasons to recover leaves lost in a season
It takes a snake five to seven days to shed its skin,
But it takes a cockerel a moment's hatching
To claim its song.

TOKI

A darkening sky is a bag holding the ghost of resistance.
I know now why some believe trees only get stronger after
Shedding leaves. You can ask a soldier back from war
Of losses, but can you feel the weight of his silence?

IN THIS LIFE

Incessant storms
Stall the clock. Yet
Matters of the heart
Are shrewd attempts
By impossibilities
To make the possible
Intangible.

DEATH OF A TYRANT

1

It happened on a day the eclipse
visited those who had grown tired

of trusting what the lips could offer
It happened after much premonitions

of heaven after hell had given birth to
prolonged talks that necessitated walks

down quiet roads and groves even the
next generation feared might turn Abuja

into a monster's hide, where heroes blinded
by the mind's failure to embrace the shine

of dreams and the streams of billions stolen
and stacked in foreign bank accounts, left

nothing but blame for the past to the next
generation and their caucus for whom justice

when sought in the aftermath of endless wars
is but a step onto paths of restitution.

2

It happened even when the clock
struck late and doors to every trusted

only offered to the injured a parliament

masked men posing as vendors of rescue
missions motivated by theatrics applauded

because they spread like wild fire the
ambition of robbers in disguise.

It happened on that day not even Wall Street
nor the World Bank could be stopped,
nor the next General in the barrack seeking

a podium to dish out a referendum announcing
his own coming to play game with the big boys,

that day in June word hit the television at home
and world news headlines, of General's death.
sage ushered in calamity in the land
and the titled turned fugitives elusive,

since an amendment to rights violated

"And the bravest thing, I think, for a writer is to face an empty page."
                --Nuruddin Farah

III

ORASHI RIVER

I jump at the opportunity
to open the doors
to your secrets.
Suitor of the weaverbird;
maiden courted by the white-tailed ant-thrush.
Your kisses at dawn the sky never gets enough;
your silence at dusk the marauders honor to keep watch.
Witness to the fisherman's reverie;
donor of grace to the swimmers unharmed.
The canoes paddled drag raffia and waterweeds
over your implosion
to write poetry in motion uninterrupted.
You of the age defying ilk!
Your paleness of skin I do not see.
Only your freshness of color,
like a snake changing skin to remain young,
teases these sneaking eyes
with voices that will not be silenced.

LAGOS LAGOON

(for Claude Ake & others)

As we take the leap off the ground
I am suddenly a child again
as I push aside an invisible curtain
to see on the rusty waters
wreckages that refuse to go away
like the crack on a car's windscreen.
And in a moment's reverie I remember
that everything alive had suddenly stopped breathing,
after news of the plane crash over
the lagoon in Lagos triggered the grimace on faces.

SOMBREIRO RIVER

All I know of you the history books have told,
with father's stories fillers.
In odd hours rebelling young men on canoe
found your presence a trusted ally,
tinkering over oil bunkering
to count their profits in a season of sorrow,
hoping the sky remains blue
until their shouts finds no room for aches.

All I know of you the history books have told.
Watery presence separating father's hometown
from neighborly lands not alien to water routes
but equally rich in oil discovered for drilling.
Lately I find your sky and soil imposing itself
on my memory for recognition
when the mind becomes dark
like a sky waiting for rain
and only yesterday's pain
tossed for the many lives lost to rival gunshots
provoked by military and police intervention
remind me again why journalism sussed
exposes traitors without names.

SONG OF FULFILLMENT

Every good thing emanates from the heart's light,
Evading darkness to challenge the prod of fate

every bad thing steals its way through eyes shut,
filling its pleasure with the delight of hurt

every sacrifice of childhood is a step up the ladder of adult-
hood, purifying the rites of passage, forging ties with aging

every victory in life comes at the expense of pain; the pregnant
mother knows this too well, and she confesses with tears upon

hearing her newborn's cry of arrival, the signature of liberation
from the combats of intensive months treading a solitary path

every joy bears the mark of tears, the cost of patience that mold's
the bleeding soldier at war into a symbol of courage

every loss in life is a gain; remember after night comes the morning,
and after sorrow springs fortitude, the breaking of new ground.

A TRIBUTE TO MOTHER

When you get there remember the nest you left behind is safe
I have wiped my eyes enough since the news of your passing
turned this home beautified by your presence into a house of silence.
The hymns have been on all day here, your favorite the most frequent,
not because it would bring you back, but because it gives us, your
beloved children, a reason to believe you will always be here with us,
in this battlefield where survival rules the affairs of men.

When you get there remember the nest you left behind is safe
for God never forgets his chosen, the children you raised with
your breast milk until they learned the ways of living from your words
and today they sit at home and remember you through laughs and tears
treasuring the nights when you gathered them at dinner table to pray
and feast on the stewed vegetables and fufu you made, even though father,
your husband, always came home late after a long day dishing out orders
like a general in an army barrack to make things moving in the seaport

When you get there remember the nest you left behind is safe
because you knew we know why you taught us what you taught us.
We who are now pressed beyond excuse to carry your name with pride
ride on the back of time and obtain the prize of sacrifice from the jaws
of fate, each day we set out in the sun desperate for success aware of the
weight of the dream cautiously kept alive by our ambition and undiminished
memories of you.

HEDE NYUIE*
-for Kofi Awoonor

The weaver bird has answered the river's call.
An empty nest now greets its legend.
Open-eyed, the sun steals a peek of messages
wrapped in words warming the heart.
This way it flew fright free,
its mission an adventure to harvest
songs for the ancestral tree.
Wheta is a place of dance,
where men live fishing for wisdom
breaking to dance, dirge and drink.
Among them the bird first learned
the mystery and beauty of flight;
among them it's believed it returned.
The weaver bird has answered the river's call,
the sun this way greets it
while its mother's house mourns,
embracing the light of its smile
each day the shadow in flight is seen
where men speak the truth to embrace love
and eschew disunity.

*ewe for safe journey
Wheta: poet's hometown

SHE

I see her every Sunday
when the testimony queue
leads to the altar.
Her feet firmly planted
before the congregation;
her eyes inwardly holding
an expression of elation.
Rwanda's pride and tears
echo in her stories,
a mother enters a room
home to nostalgia when
she pours intimately
over escaping on canoe,
baby tucked under dress,
to survive genocidal attacks.
If war had a teeth
you could see the scars
of its bites when she spoke,
reciting a continent's eulogy
from one country's tragedy.
The smell of refugee camps
she has known,
the smile of babies chuckling
to keep mothers alive
she bears in a heart not alien
to the ugliness of emptiness.
This woman not yet at midlife's
corridor, yet a witness to crimes
as old as creation tales.

AND IF I BELONG

Now that ageing has taught me to love the fading flower without
complaining, I will think again before pointing a finger at the sun.

Now that parenthood has humbled me with phases of compromise,
I will think again before positioning myself in the middle of indecisions.

There are friends and then there are friends who will be friends sometimes.
There are dreams and then there are dreams that will be elusive voluntarily.

I did not kill the rooster that deprived me of childhood initiation when called
upon to do the killing myself but was left fuming when there was nothing to kill.

A lesson kept close to the heart is twice as important as a friend treasured.
A victory earned at the loss of an irreplaceable gift opens a door to a brighter future.

Now that ageing has taught me to love the fading flower without complaining,
I will think again before pointing a finger at the sun.

WHAT SONG IN THIS WORLD IS WITHOUT SORROW?

Birds of dawn thrill the sky with adventure
until poor vision at night cuts short their pleasure.

Every child born of a woman arrives on a joyous day
with an exit day sooner or later like all flesh.

Thieves rejoice over their night's bounty,
but short memory chide the doom that stalks their path.

Plants in spring grow in the euphony of their own bliss,
until autumn brings before them a dearth gong.

Rivers may mourn their purity assaulted by flotsams,
but revel in beauty by the sun's admiration of their colors.

Winds crush whatever it pleases, scattering pollen grains
as a farmer's hand spills rice seeds in a barn full of chickens.

Amid trees felled and uprooted in nature's display of fury,
the iroko chuckles, boasting of its invincibility and immortality.

An old lion, rejected and isolated by its tribe eventually
dies upon attack by the waiting pack of hyenas that crack its bones,

making fun of the jungle's most revered resident
while waiting for another day of celebration.

WILL THEY EVER KNOW THE HARSH STRUGGLE?

Drop the titles;
the night still gives way to day.
Drop the fears;
tomorrow still waits to gather tears.
Our house of treasures
hides within its palace charlatans sung as heroes.
They have danced to the delight of their gods, and
have taken to their secret hideouts virgins for orgies.
Now the sun presents to us their nakedness,
and in their cries of innocence we note
the liars indicted by the verdict of truth.
The tail-wagging dogs rejecting their owners whistles
as they seek a place in the summit of legends.
Did the kite learn anything from its failed mission
to augment the sorrow of the mother hen?
Did the porcupine-craving lion resting under a tree
with paw pierced by tinge, bleeding, remember
the pain in victory?
Drop the titles;
the night still gives way to day.
Drop the fears;
tomorrow still waits to gather tears,
after an abundance of dreams opening
the roads to paradise and struggle.

A POEM IN CELEBRATION OF AFRICAN HISTORY

 I was once invited to read
a poem in celebration of African history,
& I took to the podium with me papers conveying in ink
the chopped heads of martyrs,
the limbs of heroes turning into dust in unmarked graves,
the rivers singing the bones and the blood of the poor,
the ghosts of warriors who died that the children may live,
the hearts of mothers who looked the nozzles of guns in the face
and spread
apart their own legs to preserve the virginity
of their infant and adolescent daughters.
& murmurs erupted to stall my show of liberation,
but the bonfire set by youth
arrested the moment with that which was crystal clear.
I craned my neck and looked for traces
of bravery from faces covered in tears,
spurred by a dislike for oppression.
Elders in discomfort abandoned their seats; echoes
ringing from dissidents eased the weight on my shoes.
A government agent waved his blood-thirsty fists at me.
"Son, you chose the wrong occasion and place to aim
bullets at folks you know nothing about, didn't you?"
asked a cranky guest, but the urgency of my calling
lashed at the audience, re-echoing
the thunder I brought with me.
Angry waves aiming for the shores of silence,
where tyranny reigned and revolution is outlawed.
 & at the end of my reading,
people with warm hearts smiled to open doors once closed.
& somewhere inside of me a voice spoke softly:
"Prepare for the harvest ahead, for you've just sowed seeds

on fertile soil, but you'll need a seasoned hunter's craftiness
& the red eyes of a nightjar to take back day from night."

GATHERING

Spare the moment a smile
if yesterday walks into us
in the middle of a debate
to turn men going crazy
into elders suddenly wise.

Our foundations of the past
were set on trials that made
no champion of a first time hunter.
Risk made the failure better with time,
so when next the mocked hunter
returns with a giant kill
much is spoken to venerate his skill.

THESE WORDS I OFFER

Our elders say even the mad man
never deceives himself by thinking
the outside of the hand is the same
as the inside. The market educates
the idle, not the room accommodating
a solitary life. It is the same
with the birds that never wrong us
with their songs. To learn the beauty
in adventure they must vacate the nest,
returning much later with experience
that spurs the longing for relocation.
These words I offer from a heart uninterested
in perturbation, but the lifting hands
to mark exhilaration.

TOMORROW'S DANCE

Even now a bright sunlight brings me ever close
To realizing she is no more, my mother. The way
Of this journey is also a whip that lashes without
Remorse. I have taken my pains quietly. Perhaps
It is only normal, seeing that there is always so
Much to do each day the sun rises and dies
to accord the punctual moon a phase so appalling,
yet Understanding. And, somewhere in this heart I
Have not stopped storing photos and voices, to
Say the least. For to bring back that which has been
Lost, one must also learn to give back to moments
The reprieve that assures the body an able participant
In tomorrow's dance.

AFTER EDWIDGE DANTICAT

The word heritage is not a pseudonym
we all use when we look back
to remember how beautiful the sun is
it is the jollof rice we eat at Chicago's African/Caribbean Interna-
tional Festival of Life
it is the soup jomou we eat for lunch on Sundays in a Haitian creole
restaurant
it is the jerk chicken with sauce and steamed cabbage we eat in
Kingston's grill house
it is the unforgettable red-onion sauteed mangu scooped with a
spoon in Santo Domingo
so we know while the head is busy kissing the sky
like Citadelle Laferrière
sacred not because it is a fortress that hides from all eyes secrets,
but because the past bears a burden brutal
like Haitian history
a harvest of tears and joys
that find a room of its own in Danticat's writings
how i loved reading we are ugly but we are here,
not because it is balderdash, but
for all the romance with pains
that cures the mind of impurities
you take the little girl's voice
then her grandmother's
then you weave a memorial
not with sadness,
but with a spirit of victory that liberates
her story
our story
the human story
Ayiti's pride

clothed by the nakedness of injustice
transformed by rebellion's curative
ah, so soothing, this remembering of our sorrows
and you are certainly right, Edwidge
death is not the end
the people we bury are going off to live somewhere else
even as we the living continue our journeys
through witness accounts also watersheds,
like Guinin's inquest
not entered at the behest
of syllogism fabricated

RITUALS

For years i've tried to be a nightingale,
hit a note funky as I dragged metaphors
across opulent Caribbean skies, to
turn tree whispers and misty scenery
into tropical jaw drawers and eye poppers.
But because peculiarity begets familiarity,
I left the nest one morning
to take on Derek Walcott's voice and
ferry across islands
salt soothed to nostalgia.
Like Braithwaite's Akan driven lines,
breathing, pausing
like the boats laying silent in Saint Lucia
on a sunny day swimmers find their way
screaming, pushing waves away
before hibernating in the kitchen,
where Callaloo crab soup, and green figs
and salt fish
-unripe banana, peeled
-sauteed with garlic, onions, celery and peppers
drain cold from the mind,
giving assurance to body and spirit,
as the curtain pushed aside
invites sun, and
the clouds pushing away
turn day into night.

AND DREAMS STILL GROW IN CHICAGO
-for Bayo

I am sitting here and I am remembering
all the faces alive with smiles,
the eyes fading with laughter,
the grin shutting up fears
when brothers and sisters jammed
the African World Festival in Chicago
and only the fanfares of a distant homeland
towered about like pines in a forest.

I am sitting here and I am remembering
them all,
the shadows of their dances
cut short by unforeseen ends,
the footprints of a legacy we
sometimes dread to claim.
How every year the number adds up
brothers and sisters in the homicide count
and my bones rattle,
fears take over the room of silence
until tears resume their walk
down the cheek.

Bayo, I still see you today
jovial, your car slowed down,
calling out the girls,
your hand hanging on the window,
driver seat pushed back
music blasting, locks
invoking Bob Marley.
You knew how to rock the gathering,

left us all exploding in laughs, until
that evening news came via TV.
Who knew it would be you that would
go down the way of the yellow tape
making a crime scene a no go area?

And ever since, every summer, I look
out for you on Sheridan Road, wishing you
would drive past the same road in your
gold-colored Lexus, as my mind is arrested
by that numbing image of you staring deep
into my eyes and the eyes of friends, while
the machine kept your heart beating
until that morning word got around that
you've answered the call from the other side.

A WAKE FOR ISAIAH

They brought him home for the final dance,
the mouthpiece of the royal palace
under shimmering sunlight.
His kinsmen strutting round the casket,
their growing voices mounting
like staff repeatedly pinned to the earth
in recognition of the revered presence.

They brought him home for the final dance,
the elderly one who arrived at the marketplace.
When he walked in the sun there were links
from his blinks to the caller of his praise name.
Ochiri, the speaker for the king
unruffled in mannerisms;
wielder of sticks clearing
imposed obstacles for the voiceless.

They brought him home for the final dance,
the chief whose belief in novel agreements
wedged open the door kept far from
the hands trembling all the time.
He has come home
surrendering his spirit
to the spirit maker
in sleep sealing an end
to the battle among the living.

He left behind footprints,
the sun named the paths.
There were echoes of tumults
but none drummed his company,

for even where the broken laughter of men
chided the sacred paths of angels,
eagles flew in admiration of the legacy exalted.

LAMENT
--for Anne

The day a letter from home announced your passing
I foraged the mind for answers, asking why a killer

would walk out of a courtroom a free man in a land also
home to well-wishers and believers of equal rights.

Through seasons of childhood and adulthood
your brief cycle of life keeps repainting this heart

with the irony of living, and because of you I have not stopped
looking at the faded photos of those taken before their time.

Today I saw a colorful bird fly across my window
as the rising sun traveled across the horizon and

I pondered the lonely walk in the wood, not to
return to deep grief, but to revisit the heart's joy

while pointing heavenward and agreeing that
you are in a peaceful place after they planted you

in the sandy soils where the birds visited with songs
that kept the children believing in dreams for tomorrow!

BOAT REGATTA ON THE CREEKS
(Port Harcourt Tourist Beach)

Twenty-three was the lucky number
as they came in droves,
proudly bearing the name
of their constituency.

Chests pumping out, mouths
& eyes wide open.
A day song louder than claps broke,
an afternoon of stunning displays on water.

Boats crafted like fish
sped with a lot of fanfare.
Drums sounding,
hands moving.

& confetti colored like the rainbow
hung over boats,
as hands, swinging forward
& backwards,

paddled along,
celebrating culture on water,
where the splendor
& grace of boats

suddenly erased fears
of shootouts
over
oil war!

TO THE POET PAYE

What song shall I sing for you this day
to cast shadows over why rivers bearing tributaries
deny me sleep?
We were born into the seaside community
where song for us was a primal urging.
Grandpa's jokes,
riddles we mimicked,
initiated us into puns.
We grew up counting the roosters' cock crow at dawn,
our lives unfolding like mats spread in the sun.
Yours was the frontal disposition;
I took my models carefully,
carving statues from the gifts of a hand I trusted
unafraid of the verdicts of spirits,
dreaded monsters of our vile heritage
who took away light
and in its place deposited sorrow.
Brother, we built our home in each other's joy
walked the night to endear the heart's fruit
to the uncertainties of life's schooling.
Often I damned what paths we crossed
in protest of your exertion of punishment
to straighten the younger sibling,
taking with me to bed at night too many bullets without a gun
Paye, Paye-ee!
Between us a coast survives,
the enchanted bridge indifferent to nostalgia
but open to the global age;
the daily remunerations of those pledging to the exodus.
What do we do when the dance arena at home is a sham
where only hands picked,

not those chosen by merit,
earn the air-conditioned office and a fat salary?
But we breathe because we dream,
our lives ceremonial clothes,
not mischievous reflections of piety
as we look ahead
and endure the weight of ageing,
aches in the bones keeping alive the travelers' dreams.
I have seen the treasures of the wonderland turn priceless.
These days I wake in the middle of the night to learn from
my palm the misfortunes of the dry season,
understanding that while you count your greying hair
in a classroom full of future adventurers,
your verse heaping in a file accumulating dust,
my burden of truth shall remain
this song I sing for you.

KOFI

When we escape night's blade
know that a harvest awaits us at sun rise.
Kofi, tell Nyidevu, Kpeti and Kove
our mother's house is on fire.
Tell them they razed a library before
the children heard the cock crow.
Tell them they poisoned the waters
before the toddlers learnt to swim.
That we are here fighting off our teeth
meat from last night's meal
while breakfast and lunch,
cold from lack of touch, attracts
the lousy flies and the stingy
house mice.

I AM

I am not the eye searching the sky for the lost sun;
I am not the displaced mother bird angry at the wind.

I am the egg that survived the raid of the tree-climbing snake;
I am the fish that fought the bait at night to swim at sunrise.

I am the honey badger that entered the beehive to dare danger;
I am the poem lost in the ocean of a poet's silence.

FOOTSTOOL FOR FOOLS

In the season of his youth he saw
a poacher reap a harvest from

a dead elephant's eulogy
made public by an eloquent sun.

Patrons in government heaped praises
on him, unmindful of the elevation in

status his solo profit brought
to a blameless rogue in the king's

palace; to the hills he returned
every morning at sunrise, his

eyes seeking the share the lions
abandoned after a sumptuous meal,

the price claimed after liars have
become content with their shares from

looting and only the anxiety for tomorrow
kept the wise restless in the republic.

This carrier of posterity's leprous
years, a footstool for fools

also sung at the gathering
of the blind.

EARTH, OIL AND WATER FEVER

(for Nnimmo, Tanure, Pious, and Ogaga)

Today I shall think hard about your words
because tomorrow's tears are today's fears

Gas flares and oil spill foreshadow death
to our natural world

Sea plants lacking exposure to sunlight die
from spilled oil exposing the cold smiles of fools

Fishermen and farmers count the days, weeks, months
and years before Shell's failed crude oil clean up

assures them a return to rivers and farmlands free
of spill threatening the fruitfulness of water and land

In the offices of the corporate world
billions of dollars multiply in oil exploitation profits,

the feat attained at the gnashing of teeth by unseen locals,
the silenced voices loyal to the moon and the sun,

each day they tell the ears willing to listen
of the agony of their wait and price of hoping...

Today I shall think hard about your words
because tomorrow's tears are today's fears

New Orleans oil spill spurred investigations and solutions, but
Bodo, Gokana oil spills left perpetrators pointing fingers

while compromised promises of clean up wait for ages,
like the solutions wished for now turning a deliberate

ploy to toy with the emotions of the aggrieved.
Some say words are cheap: true talk!

Some battles last a lifetime and here is no different,
since troubled days always face dawn and dusk

and the tired mouths fighting emotions avoid
asking any further the depressing why us!

Today I shall think hard about your words
because tomorrow's tears are today's fears.

*Bodo: a community in Gokana local government area of Rivers State, Nigeria.

THOMAS SANKARA

They spilled the rooster's blood,
Denying dawn the echo of a sacred voice.
The charmer that spread across the land
Dreams foretold.
And when night came,
They sought help from blind diviners,
The same who branded the past prophets phonies
And tagged the sacredness of their words jokes!
But epaulet and camouflage and guns
Do not only make the soldier; the mind
And the spirit led by revolution
Are also choice weapons that separate silence from might!
Thomas, brave soul whose ideas were as deep as the Nile,
Your youth left you vulnerable to ambush
In the midst of loved ones. You were
The flower that outshone the rest in the garden
And thus fell victim to the thorns that grew amongst it.
I could think up a scene of you and Cabral
Holding summit on the hoisting of flags to liberate the oppressed.
I could think up a table where you and Benazir Bhutto are seated,
Eyes on history's cracked walls, women's lib
Champs, voices
Joined in a harmony of change
To right the curses of injustice.
But the swindling wind of fate
Also brings with its rage
A column of questions unanswered.
As the heat intensifies this way, I retire
Into a room kept cold by your wise words,
Sage forced to walk down life's great hill
Before nightfall.

FRAGMENT (After EJ.)

He dreams of marrying women without hands,
The ones he could spoon feed and sing to the world
A husband's kindness under an abysmal cloud.
He warms his days with fresh plots for the finest
Of young women and trips to exotic hideouts,
Where fantasy and liberty rule over conscience.
And yet his heart is a prison yard home to birds,
Each bearing the sorrow song of the wife he eschews.

IS THERE NO END?

Tonight memory is my boat
and I want to ride it
through the storm of silence,
as I wipe away
tears dropping for the dead
after Lampedusa's boat accident
reminded me of the weight
of corpses.

Note: more than 300 migrants, mainly from Eritrea and Somali, drowned after their over-crowded dinghies sank in the Meditteranean. Some were later rescued by the coastguard and taken to the Italian island of Lampedusa. February 11, 2015.

Printed in the United States
By Bookmasters